NATIONAL FOOTBALL LEAGUE
BETWEEN THE LINES
★★★★★ READER ★★★★★

by Coach Tom Bass

SCHOLASTIC INC.

New York   Toronto   London   Auckland   Sydney
Mexico City   New Delhi   Hong Kong   Buenos Aires

With love to my Grandchildren Sara, Robby, Tucker and Delilah Grace

All photos © Getty Images.
Front Cover (left to right): Otto Greule Jr.; Otto Greule Jr.; Jonathan Daniel
Back Cover (left to right): Otto Greule Jr.; Greg Flume; Steve Hutchinson
Interior: (5) Chris Graythen; (8) Doug Pensinger, Doug Pensinger, Jonathan Daniel; (11) Brian Bahr, Doug Pensinger; (13) Otto Greule Jr.; (14) Otto Greule Jr., Jeff Gross; (17) Andy Lyons, Lisa Blumenfeld; (19) Jed Jacobsohn; (20) Doug Benc, Jonathan Daniel; (23) Greg Flume, Jonathan Daniel; (25) Doug Benc; (26) Brain Behr, Jim McIsaac (30) Tom Pidgeon, Andy Lyons, Brendan Smialowski, Jonathan Daniel, Eliot J. Schechter

ISBN-13: 978-0-439-92455-9
ISBN-10: 0-439-92455-3

Published by Scholastic Inc.
SCHOLASTIC and associated logos are trademarks and/or registered trademarks of Scholastic Inc.

12 11 10 9 8 7 6 5 4   8 9 10 11/0

Designed by Kim Brown
Printed in the U.S.A.
First Scholastic printing, August 2007

Learning the Positions

Learning about the different positions on a football team is a good place to start if you want to play the game. Football teams are made up of the **offense** (the players with the ball), the **defense** (the players without the ball), and **special teams** (the players involved with the kicking game).

Football is a team sport, and every position on the team is important. To help you pick the best position for you, we will first look at the physical characteristics and job responsibilities of the position. Then we will highlight NFL players who have shown outstanding ability at those positions.

Naming the Offensive Positions

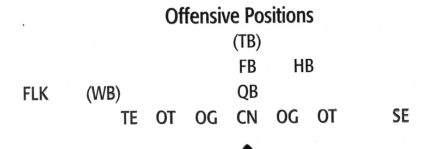

Offensive Positions

The *offensive line* has five players: the center (CN), 2 guards (OG) on either side of the center (CN), and 2 tackles (OT) on either side of the guards.

The *offensive backfield* has three players: the quarterback (QB), the fullback (FB), and the halfback (HB)/tailback (TB).

There are three *offensive receivers*: the tight end (TE) on the outside of a tackle (OT), the flanker (FLK)/wing back (WB) on the outside of the tight end (TE), and the split end (SE) split wide from a tackle (OT).

The wing back (WB) position is often included as part of the backfield grouping. Many coaches think of the quarterback (QB) position as a special "group" by itself.

Naming the Defensive Positions

Defensive Positions

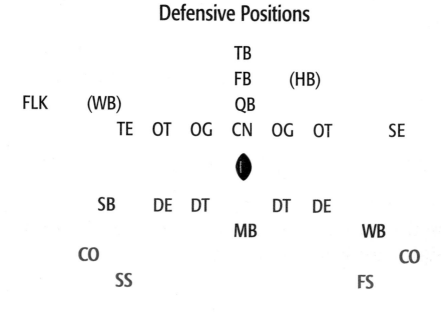

The defensive team is made up of three groups. Unlike the offense, the number of players in each group on the defensive team can vary based on the kind of defense your coach chooses.

The *defensive line* has either three, four, five, or six players: the 2 tackles (DT) line up in front of the OGs, and 2 ends (DE) line up on the outside of the tackles (DT). If a defensive lineman lines up in front of the center (CN), he is called the nose tackle (NT).

The *linebackers* are made up of two, three, or four players: the middle backer (MB) lines up off the line in front of an OG, the strong side backer (SB) lines up on the line in front of the tight end (TE), and the weak side backer (WB) lines up off the line on the same side as the split end (SE).

The *defensive backs* are made up of three, four, or five players: the two corners (CO) line up off the line in front of the flanker (FLK) and split end (SE), the strong safety (SS) lines up off the line on the same side as the tight end (TE), and the free safety (FS) lines up off the line on the same side as the split end (SE).

Naming the Special Teams Positions

Most of the players who participate in any phase of the kicking game will be offensive or defensive players. Specialists are also needed for certain positions on special teams.

Point After Touchdown (PAT) And
Field Goal (FG) — 3 Players

TE   OT   OG   SN   OG   OT   TE

WB   WB

H

PK

When the team is kicking an extra point, that is, point after touchdown (PAT), or field goal (FG), three players have special jobs: the short snapper (SN), the holder (H), and the placekicker (PK). The other eight players are blockers.

KICKOFF TEAM — 1 PLAYER

L5   L4   L3   L2   L1   R1   R2   R3   R4   R5

K

When a team is kicking off at the beginning of each half and after a team has scored, only the kicker (K) has a special job. The other ten players are tacklers.

PUNT TEAM – 2 PLAYERS

LG   LT LG LN RG RT   RG

        LW   RW

                                FB

              P

When the team doesn't make a first down and they have to punt, two players have special jobs: the long snapper (LN) and the punter (P). The other nine players block if needed and then become tacklers once the ball is kicked.

Return Team Specialist

Anytime a team is receiving a kick, one or two players will line up deep off the line and return the kick. The other players will rush the kicker and then serve as blockers for the kickoff returner (KR).

CHAPTER ONE
Offensive Line

The offensive line is made up of five players: a center (CN), two guards (OG), and two tackles (OT). Every successful team has a good offensive line. It does not matter how talented the quarterback (QB), running backs (see chapter three), or receivers are if the offensive line does not do its job. Being an offensive lineman is one of the most important positions on the team.

Responsibilities

When the offense is running the ball, the offensive line is expected to open holes for the ball carrier. To do this, you have to stop the charge of the defensive player, push him back off the line, and turn him away from the path of the ball carrier.

Your coach will teach you the techniques you have to master for the various blocks you will use to stop the defensive players, and then you will practice them over and over.

On pass plays, the job of the offensive lineman is to protect the quarterback (QB) until he has an opportunity to throw the ball. This means that you must stop the rush of the defensive player and force him away from where the quarterback (QB) is setting up to throw.

If you play offensive center (CN), you also need to correctly snap the ball to the quarterback (QB) to start every play. Every offensive play starts with an exchange of the ball from the center to the quarterback. Making this exchange occur at the exact moment the play is supposed to begin is the number one responsibility for a center.

Characteristics

Offensive linemen must be strong, have good balance, and be quick when running short distances. Speed in a forty-yard dash is not nearly as important as your ability to quickly move from your stance to successfully block a defensive player on a run or pass play.

In addition, you must be smart, understand each play, know whom to block and which block to use, and learn to work as part of a smooth unit with your other offensive linemen.

Lining Up

OT   OG   CN   OG   OT

PLAYERS TO WATCH

OT Jonathan Ogden #75

Plays the difficult position of left tackle for the Baltimore Ravens.

OG Steve Hutchinson #78

Has great speed, strength, and balance. Plays left guard for the Minnesota Vikings.

CN Olin Kreutz #57

A smart, outstanding offensive center for the Chicago Bears.

Quarterback

The quarterback (QB) position is a backfield position on the offensive team. When playing quarterback, you are the leader of the offense. This is one of the most exciting and challenging positions because of the many different skills and techniques you must learn. On each and every offensive play, you will start the play, touch the ball, and be part of the play.

Responsibilities

When you play quarterback, prior to the start of any offensive play, you are responsible for getting your team in a huddle; telling them the formation, the play, and the snap count; breaking the huddle; and making certain they are lined up correctly on the line of scrimmage. Then you must call out the cadence, start the play, receive the ball from the center, and carry out your assignment for the play. One of your most important jobs is to make sure that you get the ball from the center at the start of every play.

On a running play, you will need to take the snap and then either hand, pitch, or toss the ball to the designated ball carrier. On some plays, you may be asked to run the ball yourself. Once you have successfully given the ball to another player, you will then be asked to set up, to pass, or to carry out a fake away from the path of the ball carrier.

On a pass play, you will have to set up correctly, pick out the appropriate receiver, and then deliver the ball to that receiver. If no receiver is open, you will need to run with the ball or throw the ball out of bounds.

Characteristics

As a quarterback, you need the ability to run the ball when necessary and the physical skill to pass the ball. You must have a good passing technique that allows you to throw with accuracy to varying distances, from the line of scrimmage, to all of your receivers.

You will need to understand the offense, be a leader on the field, and have the ability to motivate the other ten offensive players and direct them to successfully move the ball down the field and score.

Lining Up

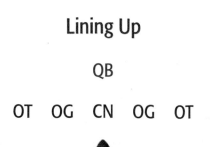

QB

OT   OG   CN   OG   OT

PLAYERS TO WATCH

QB Peyton Manning #18

Makes good decisions, has a strong arm, and is
an excellent leader for the Indianapolis Colts.

QB Michael Vick #7

Combines accurate passing and excellent running ability,
making him a double threat for the Atlanta Falcons.

Running Back

The offensive backfield is normally made up of three players: a quarterback (QB), a fullback (FB), and a halfback (HB)/tailback (TB). The fullback and halfback are also called running backs. One of the most exciting things a running back can do is to receive the ball from the quarterback, break through the line, and make a first down or score a touchdown.

Responsibilities

As a halfback, you will probably be the ball carrier on running plays. Your job will be to receive the ball from the quarterback, secure the ball, and gain as many yards as you can. On plays where the fullback carries the ball, you may be asked to block or to fake carrying the ball in the other direction.

A fullback performs the same tasks whether he is carrying the ball or blocking.

On any pass play, both the halfback and the fullback may be required to stay in the backfield and block to protect the quarterback or to run a designated pass route where they must be prepared to catch the ball and run with it after the catch.

Characteristics

As a halfback, you need speed, quickness, and the ability to change direction. You need to run good pass routes, be a good receiver, and have the toughness to carry and protect the ball.

When you play fullback you need to be strong, be a good blocker, and run with power when you carry the ball.

Lining Up

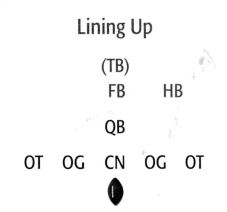

```
              (TB)
              FB      HB

              QB

  OT   OG   CN   OG   OT
```

PLAYERS TO WATCH

RB Shaun Alexander #37

Strong, fast, powerful running back for the Seattle Seahawks.

RB LaDainian Tomlinson #21

Elusive runner, excellent receiver, and good
blocker for the San Diego Chargers.

Receivers and Tight End

As a wide receiver (FLK or SE), you get the chance to make big plays for your offense by catching a short pass and then breaking free for a big gain or by streaking past a defensive back and pulling in a long pass. As a tight end (TE), you will be asked to be a blocker on run plays and a receiver on pass plays.

Responsibilities

On all running plays, the receiver and/or tight end has the job of blocking for the ball carrier. If you are the receiver (a flanker or a split end), you will usually be asked to block a defensive back, either a safety or a defensive corner. As a tight end, you will usually be blocking a linebacker or defensive end off the line of scrimmage and away from the path of the ball carrier.

When the offense is throwing the ball, your job as a wide receiver or tight end is to run the pass route called in the huddle by sprinting off the line of scrimmage to a designated area of the field. You should try to create distance from the defensive player covering you, get open, and make the catch thrown from the quarterback.

Characteristics

When you play wide receiver, you can be a smaller player. You will need good speed to get open, agility to run your routes, good hand–eye coordination to make the catch, and the ability to run with the ball after making the catch.

As a tight end, you will need the size, strength, and balance of an offensive lineman to be an effective blocker, plus the receiving skills of a wide receiver.

Both the receivers and tight end need to have good hands and a determination to catch every ball thrown to them.

Lining Up

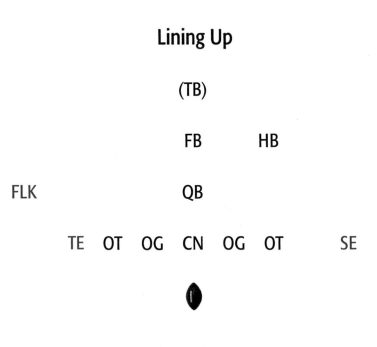

PLAYERS TO WATCH

WR Marvin Harrison #88

Exceptional route runner with sure hands for the Indianapolis Colts.

TE Antonio Gates #85

Fast, smooth routes, great agility, and good
hands for the San Diego Chargers.

Defensive Line

The defensive line can be made up of three, four, or six defensive tackles (DT) and ends (DE). Playing on the defensive line is fun and gives you the opportunity to get into the action on every play, whether the other team's offense is trying to run or pass the ball.

Responsibilities

As a defensive lineman, when the offense runs the ball, your job will be to charge across the line at the start of the play, identify the player who is blocking you, stop the blocker and push him away, locate the ball carrier, move to him, and be part of the tackle.

When the offense attempts to pass the ball, you then get to rush the quarterback. On the snap, you need to rush across the line, avoid the offensive player blocking you, pressure the quarterback to throw early, try to deflect the ball, and best of all get a sack by tackling the quarterback before he can throw.

Characteristics

When you play on the defensive line, you need to be strong in the legs, upper body, arms, and shoulders. You need quick reactions, quick movement in a short area, and the determination to try to reach the ball carrier on every play.

Lining Up

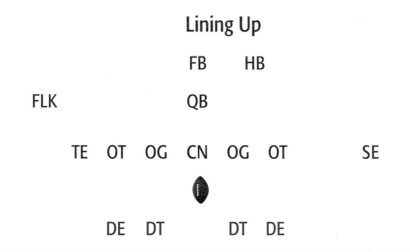

FB   HB

FLK   QB

TE   OT   OG   CN   OG   OT   SE

DE   DT   DT   DE

PLAYERS TO WATCH

DE Michael Strahan #92

Strong versus the run and excellent pass
rusher for the New York Giants.

DT Tommie Harris #91

Big, strong, quick inside lineman for the Chicago Bears.

CHAPTER SIX
Linebackers

A defense may use two, three, four, or even five linebackers in a game. Linebackers have to be able to stop the running plays like a defensive lineman, while playing pass defense like a defensive back. A linebacker sees *lots* of action. The defense on the next page features three linebackers – a middle backer (MB), a weak side backer (WB), and a strong side backer (SB).

Responsibilities

As a linebacker, you have the job of determining if the offense is running or passing the ball the instant the play begins.

On running plays, you move toward the line of scrimmage; determine who is assigned to block you; stop, defeat, or avoid the blocker; move away from the blocker and toward the ball carrier; and make the tackle on the ball carrier. If you are an outside linebacker, you may be asked to steer the ball carrier back to the center of the field to your teammates.

When you play linebacker and the offense attempts to pass the ball, you may be asked to rush the quarterback. On other plays, you will run and cover a receiver, often a running back, all over the field if you are playing a man-to-man pass coverage. You may even have to sprint to a designated area of the field, set up, and be ready to react when the ball is thrown if you are playing a zone pass defense.

Characteristics

As a linebacker, you should be smart and love to play the game. You will need to be strong, especially in the upper body, be able to defeat offensive blockers, and have good speed and quickness. It is important that you have a desire to be in on every tackle. Finally, you should have good hand–eye coordination, so you can make an interception, plus the skills necessary to run with the ball.

Lining Up

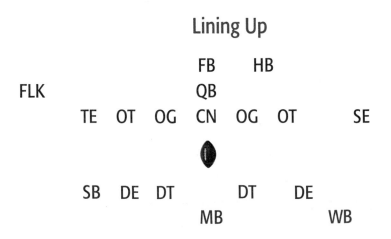

PLAYERS TO WATCH

OLB Joey Porter #55

Strong, quick, excellent against the run or
pass for the Pittsburgh Steelers.

MLB Brian Urlacher #54

Great instincts, hard aggressive
tackler, and leader of the defense for the Chicago Bears.

CHAPTER SEVEN
Defensive Backs

The defensive backs usually consist of three or four players. When you play as a defensive back, you will have the challenge of being the last line of defense on running and pass plays. On the next page is a four-player defensive back alignment — two corners (CO), a strong safety (SS), and a free safety (FS).

Responsibilities

As a defensive back, you should be able to identify and avoid any offensive blocker, move quickly to the ball carrier, and then be part of the tackle.

On plays where the offense attempts to pass, you will need to be able to cover any receiver assigned to you if it is a man-to-man coverage or to drop into a designated area of the field when playing a zone pass defense. When the ball is thrown, you will need to try to deflect or intercept the pass or make a tackle if the receiver catches the ball. After an interception, you need good running skills to carry the ball.

Characteristics

As a defensive back, you need good speed to run with the wide receivers. You must be smart, love competition, and be able to focus on the next play, not dwelling on the result of the previous play. As the last person between a ball carrier and the goal line, you need to be a willing and sure tackler. Finally, you should have good hand–eye coordination so you can make an interception.

Lining Up

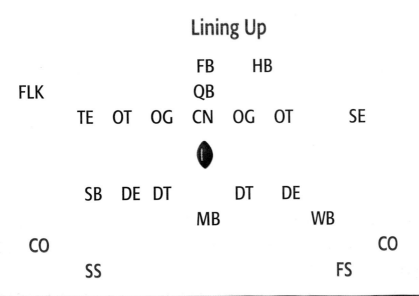

FB   HB

FLK   QB

TE OT OG CN OG OT   SE

SB DE DT   DT DE

MB   WB

CO   CO

SS   FS

PLAYERS TO WATCH

CO   Champ Bailey #24

Excellent cover corner with sure tackling skills
for the Denver Broncos.

SS   Troy Polamalu #43

Great range, excellent on blitz, and an aggressive
hard tackler for the Pittsburgh Steelers.

Specialists

Often one third of a game's plays, and many of the team's offensive and defensive players, will be involved in either kicking or receiving kicks. Because of the opportunity to score points, plus creating field position change, your role as a specialist is extremely important and exciting.

On kicking teams you may be asked to block, cover, and tackle, while on return teams your challenge may include rushing the kicker and then blocking for your teammate who is returning the kick.

Diagrams in the introduction show where the specialists should line up.

Responsibilities

PAT/FG Team

The Short Snapper (SN) needs to be able to accurately snap the ball back through his legs seven yards to the holder, and then help block until the ball is kicked.

The Holder (H) sets up next to the tee, checks to see that the kicker is ready, signals the center that the kicker is ready, catches the snap, and correctly places the ball on the tee for the kicker. If there is a bad snap from the center, you must try to run or pass the ball for a first down or score.

The job of the Placekicker (PK) is to line up properly, signal the holder that you are ready, take the proper approach to the tee and ball, and correctly kick the ball through the uprights.

Kickoff Team

The Kicker (K) needs to correctly place the ball on the tee, line up properly, take the correct approach to the tee and ball, and then kick the ball as far down the field as you can. After the kick, you should be a safety and position yourself to make a tackle on the return player if he breaks through.

Punt Team

The Long Snapper (LN) needs to be able to accurately snap the ball back through his legs to the punter (10–15 yards), help block until the ball is kicked, and then run down the field to help make the tackle on any player returning the punt.

The Punter (P) must line up properly, signal the center you are ready for the snap, catch the snap, take the appropriate steps, and correctly punt the ball as far down the field as you can. After the punt, you should become a safety on one half of the field and position yourself to make a tackle on the return player if he breaks through.

Kick Return

The Punt Returner's (PR) job is to line up a particular distance from the line of scrimmage based on the punter's ability and your position on the field, see the ball as it leaves the punter's foot, move in front of the ball in flight, decide to fair catch and secure the punt or return the punt as far as possible, or let the punt roll dead.

The Kickoff Returner (KR) lines up at a particular distance down the field based on the kicker's ability, sees the ball as it comes off the tee, moves in front of the flight of the ball, makes the catch, and returns the ball up the field as far as possible.

Characteristics

The Short and Long Snappers each need the skill to center and then snap the ball back between their legs, the strength to be a blocker, the speed to run downfield on a punt, and the agility to tackle the return player.

The Holder must have good hands, the agility to place the ball on the tee, and the physical skill to run or pass the ball if there is a bad snap.

The Placekicker should have a strong leg and be able to kick the ball off the ground or tee from a hold through the uprights and over the crossbar.

The Kicker [kickoff] should have a strong leg and be able to kick the ball off the tee to the left, center, and right areas of the field, plus the physical ability to make a tackle when necessary.

The Punter should have good hands to catch the snap, a strong leg to make the kick, and the ability to punt the ball correctly, plus the physical ability to make a tackle when necessary.

The Kick Return Players need good hands to make the catch, the ability to make quick decisions and to focus on the ball, the determination to return the kick, and the running skills to dodge tacklers as you bring the ball back up the field.

PLAYERS TO WATCH

LONG SNAPPER
Brad St. Louis #48

Fast, accurate snapper who covers and tackles for the Cincinnati Bengals.

PLACEKICKER
Adam Vinatieri #4

Accurate kicker who makes game-winning kicks under pressure for the Indianapolis Colts.

PUNTER
Josh Miller #8

Excellent punter for distance and accuracy for the New England Patriots.

KICKOFF RETURN
Maurice Hicks #43

Shows great speed, determination, and running ability when returning kickoffs for the San Francisco 49ers.

PUNT RETURN
Wes Welker #83

Wes Welker did such a good job returning punts for Miami last year that the Patriots traded for him this season.